Original title:
Through the Front Door, Into the Soul

Copyright © 2025 Creative Arts Management OÜ
All rights reserved.

Author: George Mercer
ISBN HARDBACK: 978-1-80587-071-5
ISBN PAPERBACK: 978-1-80587-541-3

Curved Corners of the Mind

In a house where thoughts reside,
The cat runs, my thoughts collide.
I trip over shoes, what a sight,
Laughter echoes in morning light.

Old clocks tick to a silly tune,
I dance with shadows, oh, how they swoon!
Coffee spills with every cheer,
Walls giggle, 'It's good to be here!'

Embracing the Unfamiliar

A fridge hums secrets, quite a chat,
I swear I just saw my pet cat spat.
Grapes play hide and seek in my bowl,
What a funny game, oh, what a goal!

Sandwiches gossip in their crusty way,
My socks run off, and then they play.
Each corner hides a quirky surprise,
Smiles bubble up, oh what a prize.

Portraits on the Passageway

On walls hang smiles, all the same,
A family photo? What a great game!
My brother's hair looks like a mop,
I can't stop giggling, can't make it stop!

The hallway twists like a twisty straw,
Maybe a giraffe will take a paw?
This carpet laughs, a bright cheery hue,
I wonder if it knows my next 'who?'

The Key to Forgotten Dreams

A key made of jelly, what a delight,
Unlocks the dreams that dance at night.
A hot dog dreams of being a star,
While I wonder where all my socks are!

In a closet, a ghost sings a tune,
About lost shoes and a blue balloon.
Laughter spills, secrets untold,
In this funny world, life's a bright fold.

The Soft Light of Introspection

A mirror flickers, reflecting my grin,
Caught in the fabric of where I've been.
Serious thoughts, like socks in a drawer,
They match up seldom, but who keeps score?

A pillow whispers secrets, too tight to share,
In cozy corners, I trip on despair.
Light-hearted laughter dances in the air,
I grunt, I chuckle, my worries laid bare.

Moments Captured in the Hall

Photos on walls, they wiggle and sway,
Each frame a jest, come join the play.
Grandma's wig, a hat on my cat,
In every snapshot, a laugh, a spat.

The hallway echoes tales of delight,
The vacuum cleaner's an unexpected fright.
Ticking clocks giggle, they skip and race,
Reminders that life is a zany space.

Unfolding Stories of the Heart

With every beat, a fresh punchline springs,
Balloons of laughter, oh how it stings!
Heartbeats drumming, a joyful parade,
While socks get lost in the laundry brigade.

Frog on the porch croaks a silly tune,
It's hard to feel gloom under the moon.
They say love's a puzzle, with pieces amissing,
Yet here I am, giggling and kissing!

The Corridor of Reverie

In dreams I tiptoe, sneaking a peek,
Hoping my socks will reschedule this week.
The corridor stretches, a comical sight,
Each door a new quirk, oh what a fright!

Room 101 holds a chattering shoe,
While Room 102 boasts a dance for two.
In this wacky space where sounds come to play,
I find giggles and grins brighten my day.

Where Souls Meet

In a café where shadows wiggle,
And souls sip tea, trying to giggle.
A cat walks in, wearing a hat,
Declaring loudly, 'Where's my mat?'

The barista whispers spells with steam,
While spirits plot a quirky dream.
A dance breaks out, chairs start to slide,
As everyone joins, there's nowhere to hide.

Inside the Whispering Walls

In a house where voices peek,
Walls gossip softly, secrets speak.
A squirrel scurries, taking a stroll,
Climbing high, that's his sole goal.

The pictures nod, with eyes so wide,
As if they know what secrets hide.
With laughter echoing down the hall,
Who knew wood could have such a ball?

A Doorway to Dreams

A portal shines with colors bright,
Inviting all to join the flight.
A jester jumps, then trips and rolls,
Declaring, 'Welcome, dreamer souls!'

Unicorns stroll and cake floats by,
Rubber ducks dance, oh my, oh my!
With laughter ringing through the night,
The world turns strange, a pure delight.

Entrances to Eternity

A door stands tall, painted in blue,
Behind it whispers, 'What's your view?'
A dragon yawns and takes a seat,
While poets try to find their beat.

A troll plays chess with a fairy queen,
In a game where nothing's as it seems.
Each move a giggle, each piece a cheer,
Who knew eternity would be so dear?

Inward Steps of Introspection

I tiptoe softly, don't want to peek,
Do I smell cookies or week-old fleece?
In the hallway, there's a poster of a cat,
Wearing sunglasses, just chilling on a mat.

The fridge is humming, it's starting to sing,
What's left in there, oh the joy it can bring!
A strange concoction, possibly cheese,
Or maybe a science experiment that sneezes.

Secrets Beneath the Welcome Mat

Lift the mat, what will I find?
A key to a treasure or a muddy rind?
Perhaps a sock that traveled the world,
Or a note from a ghost, slightly unfurled.

It's cozy here, with secrets to share,
Like who left said sock - maybe a bear?
Perhaps some dust bunnies, plotting their raid,
On forgotten snacks that were never made.

The Portal Within

Open your mind like a pizza box,
Remember the toppings? What a paradox!
This slice of thought, cheesy and wide,
Slips out of reach with each silly stride.

I trip over laughter, joy in my wake,
Like Uncle Joe's jokes, a classic mistake.
Every giggle, a step through the door,
Into a land where we're all like before.

Rooms of the Untold

Behind closed doors, what fun might we see?
A dance party with old shoes, just for me!
In the corner, a cat breaks it down,
With moves so wild, it should wear a crown.

Curiosity peeks, like a mouse on a spree,
What resides in the closet, oh let it be!
A wizard's hat or a pile of fluff,
In these rooms of wonder, it's all quite enough!

The Veil of the Ordinary

Behind each door, a tale unfolds,
A sock parade, as life beholds.
The garden gnome, a wise old sage,
Critiques my plants, all the rage.

Fridge magnets boast, with flair and pride,
Of places I've been, no time to hide.
Yet behind the scenes, the cat does plot,
To steal my lunch, in its own sweet spot.

Steps into the Depths of Being

As I trudge down the carpeted path,
Barefoot on Legos, inciting wrath.
Each picture frame, a curious stare,
Do they judge my cleaning, or lack of care?

The coffee pot hums a morning tune,
Dancing with spills, around the afternoon.
In every creak, a secret's laid,
A sandwich thief in Tupperware's shade.

Luminescence Beyond the Threshold

The light bulb flickers, as if to jest,
Mocking my choice of pajama dress.
I tiptoe past, in a half-hearted dash,
Mismatched socks in a stylish clash.

The hallway's length, a runway rare,
Where echoes of laughter prance in air.
A mop's lurking shadow, with fearsome intent,
It frightens the cat, that's heaven-sent.

Shadows Dancing in the Hallway

In hallways where light and shadow meet,
Dust bunnies churn in a silent beat.
With every step, my knees do creak,
An elderly choir that's far from meek.

Socks on the stairs, a slippery fate,
Each reach for balance, an exercise great!
Yet despite the chaos, I laugh with glee,
For this silly mess feels just like me.

The Hidden Door of Perception

In a house full of junk, I found some cheese,
A door behind the bookshelf, with a creak it frees.
Don't ask who lives there, it might make you cringe,
A garden of socks awaits, on a broken hinge.

With a welcome mat that reads 'Please tread with care',
The cat wears a hat, pretending to stare.
A treasure trove of lost socks, mismatched and bold,
Where the stories of missing shoes are lovingly told.

The Interlude of Essence

I opened a drawer that hadn't seen light,
In search of the pair, my left shoe took flight.
An interlude of chaos in each little space,
A dance of the dust bunnies, quick in their race.

When I tried to escape, I tripped over a pen,
It rolled with a jingle, lights blinked, then—hen!
I burst through the laughter painted on walls,
Wondering if sanity still funnily calls.

Enveloping the Fragile Being

Wrapped in a blanket that's seen better days,
I ponder the meaning, lost in a haze.
The toaster is buzzing, it's writing a song,
While the fridge tells a joke—it's been waiting too long.

A fragile being sipping a cup of old tea,
With thoughts like confetti—come dance here with me!
The walls start to giggle, the floorboards all sway,
In this sanctuary where nonsense holds sway.

Safeguarding the Inner Glow

Oh, look, a cupboard that's bursting with flair,
It guards mismatched spoons like they're treasures rare.
Each fork has a story, each knife feels alive,
They gossip and giggle, in joy they thrive.

As the light spills in, casting shadows so tall,
I chuckle at slippers that seem to have brawl.
Here, the glow isn't just warmth, but a silly parade,
Safeguarding laughter in the friendships we've made.

Tapestries of Hidden Lives

In the hall where secrets hide,
A sock puppet wants to bide.
The cat pretends it's not a spy,
While the toaster watches with a sigh.

Shadows mingle, whispers fly,
A garden gnome hears every lie.
As curtains twitch in laughter's grace,
The floorboards groan in their embrace.

Each picture frame has tales to share,
Of awkward dances and wild hair.
With every knock, a new charade,
The clock ticks on, never afraid.

So come inside, don your best face,
In this tapestry, find your place.
For even walls with stories grand,
Will giggle softly at your stand.

The Dance of Invitations

A paper plane took flight askew,
Inviting chaos, isn't that new?
The sofa beckons with a grin,
As potted plants break out in spin.

The doorbell rings, who could it be?
A hilarious twist of fate, you'll see!
With each new guest, a giggle grows,
Like silly hats that everyone knows.

The fridge hums tunes of meals past,
While pizza crusts dream of being cast.
And every chair has stories wide,
Of dance-off nights and jokes untried.

So gather round, don't hesitate,
For every knock holds fun-filled fate.
In this dance of cheerful calls,
You'll find confetti in the walls.

The Treasures of a Warm Embrace

Every hug is a pirate's stash,
With laughter and giggles in a splash.
The couch offers its softest throne,
While fresh-baked cookies slyly moan.

A game of tag on carpeted seas,
With tickles and squeals riding the breeze.
The walls are lined with silly frames,
Each smiling face has funny names.

In this treasure where joy convenes,
A rubber chicken sneaks in between.
Swapping stories of gaffes and slips,
As everyone takes joyful dips.

So dive right in, it's never late,
To find the warmth that friends create.
In this embrace, let love's glow blaze,
For life's huge stage is full of praise.

Keys to the Heart's Chamber

A jangling keychain bids me enter,
Unlocking giggles from the corner center.
Every twist reveals a quirky nook,
Where socks dance madly and cookies look.

In the drawer, a pile of lost dreams,
A hat with feathers, or so it seems.
A treasure chest filled with silly notes,
Each one a tale that simply floats.

Unveiling the Inner Sanctum

Behind the curtain, a riot unfolds,
Where laughter echoes, and chaos molds.
A pet goldfish, sporting a tiny hat,
Floats by, giving advice on where it's at.

Crumpets and tea from an ancient pot,
Turned into jester with one little shot.
The walls are painted with puns and cheer,
Each brushstroke whispers, 'Come closer, my dear!'

Greeted by the Spirit

A ghostly giggle drifts through the air,
Wearing mismatched socks, in a colorful flair.
It tickles the senses, makes shadows dance,
Inviting the brave for a dizzying trance.

With tea made of giggles and biscuits of dreams,
We toast to the weirdness, or so it seems.
Laughter erupts as the spirit spins,
In this strange place, everyone wins!

The Passage Within

Down a wiggly hallway that never ends,
Where jellybeans giggle and candy bends.
Each step is a jig, a carnival song,
The walls hum with joy, won't take long.

A mirror that dances, a floor that shakes,
Invites you to laugh, oh, for goodness' sakes!
And here in this maze of whimsy and fun,
We celebrate life until the day is done.

Secrets Beneath the Welcome

There's a cat that guards the hall,
With a stare that can make me stall.
He knows of secrets tucked away,
Like why my socks don't match today.

The creaky floorboards start to sing,
Of all the joys that chaos brings.
Spilled cereal makes a fine design,
Our house is messy, but that's just fine.

Behind the coat rack lives a ghost,
Whose jokes about dust are what I love most.
It chuckles softly when guests arrive,
Making our home feel very alive.

So if you knock and hear a cheer,
Just know there's laughter waiting near.
Unravel tales where joy's the goal,
Here lies the whimsy of the soul.

Echoes of the Hidden Nest

In the attic where old toys reside,
A wooden horse does a gentle glide.
He whispers tales, quite absurd,
About a cat who thinks he's a bird.

Under the stairs, take care, my friend,
A sock monster waits, it won't pretend.
It juggles oddities with delight,
Wearing mismatched shoes, quite a sight!

The fridge hums rhythms of delight,
Weekly leftovers await in flight.
Tupperware dreams of being a feast,
But all they do is beckon the least.

So join me now, embrace the quirk,
In this sanctuary where joys lurk.
With each odd nook, a giggle steals,
Echoes of laughter, warmth, and feels.

Entrance to the Inner Realm

As you step in, the air grows thick,
With scents of cookies baked with a trick.
The cookie jar laughs, 'Take a bite!'
But then it moans, 'You might get tight!'

A mirror whispers silly jokes,
Reflecting all the chubby folks.
It claims it's honest, doesn't lie,
Except for hairs that refuse to comply.

The living room's a circus show,
With pillows bouncing, to and fro.
Laughter erupts with every leap,
As the dog dreams of chasing sheep.

So open wide the gates of cheer,
This inner realm has nothing to fear.
With giggles echoing from each wall,
Embrace the whimsy, joy, and all.

A Doorway to Essence

Here lies the door painted bright pink,
Beyond it's chaos, the kitchen sink.
It gurgles softly, a bubbling tease,
'Teaday, my friend, who brewed the cheese?'

The coat rack shivers, telling lies,
Of days when snowflakes kissed the skies.
Yet here it hangs, with coats galore,
And a hat proclaiming 'I am for four!'

In the corner lurks a potted plant,
Whispering tales that make me chant.
It sways and sings a green delight,
Inviting all to stay the night.

So linger here, and find your place,
In a jumbled jumble, life's embrace.
Every laugh a secret scroll,
A doorway here reveals the soul.

First Step into the Depths

I tiptoe in, my socks are bright,
A cat appears, a furry fright.
It stares at me with eyes aglow,
As if to say, "Now, where'd you go?"

I trip on shoes, they form a pile,
A mountain high, it makes me smile.
Heartbeat races, what's inside?
Perhaps old snacks I'll try to hide.

A mirror greets me, grinning back,
With toothpaste smudged, a face quite whack.
I laugh aloud, a sneaky peek,
To enter here, I'll need some cheek.

With every step, the echoes cheer,
"Welcome back! We've missed you here!"
And as I plunge, I wade through dreams,
Where silly socks can burst in seams.

Embracing the Inner Light

I found a glow beneath the bed,
A flashlight dead, yet hope instead.
I squint my eyes, oh what a sight,
A rogue sock dance, a pure delight!

Reflective surfaces all around,
In cereal bowls, great sights I found.
With every sip of evening's brew,
My soul took flight, in pinkish hue.

Through dusty corners, treasures pile,
A rubber duck with a cheeky smile.
It quacks a tune I can't resist,
"Join the party!" with a twist.

The light I sought was just a glare,
In kitchen drawers, and I don't care.
For laughter lives where shadows dwell,
A joyful heart, the best of spells.

The Threshold of Reflection

At the entrance, doubts in tow,
I'm ready now, to smile and glow.
The mirror winks, does it know me?
Or is it just a ghostly spree?

I ponder hard, a silly frown,
As old clothes laugh, they call me clown.
Through frames and dust, the past appears,
With every step, it brings me cheers.

A dance of socks on wooden floors,
They've staged a play with just two doors.
I lose my thoughts, I lose my weight,
In laughable antics, I celebrate.

I finally see the truth unfold,
Life's not a tale that's always told.
Just tricky hits and funny quirks,
Revealing joy in all its works.

Hushed Conversations in the Foyer

In corners here, the whispers creep,
A rogue broom speaks, while others sleep.
The clocks are giggling, ticking slow,
Insights shared about the dough.

The coats debate on who's the best,
A velvet cape or striped-request.
They chat away, like friends so dear,
While I just chuckle, never fear.

The shoes all gather for a sneak,
They ponder life and what we seek.
"Will she wear us or leave us be?"
I wink, "Just wait, your fate's with me!"

With each hello and every grin,
I walk the path where laughs begin.
In quiet spaces, secrets share,
A foyer full of jokes and flair.

Soft Footfalls in the Heartspace

A squirrel taps lightly on my floor,
Chasing crumbs, it takes a tour.
It wiggles, giggles, steals the show,
I trip on laughter, oh no, oh no!

In the kitchen, it stirs the pot,
Uninvited guest, it loves the lot.
I try to shoo it, but it won't flee,
"Hey buddy, save some crumbs for me!"

With tiny paws and a twitching tail,
It dances round, a nutty trail.
While I sip tea, it eyes my snack,
This sneaky friend, no turning back!

As sunset paints the sky with glee,
Our dance of joy, just squirrel and me.
The heartspace laughs, love's playful tune,
Who knew a squirrel could light up the room?

Paths Unwritten within the Walls

In every nook, a secret dwells,
Behind the cupboards, a tale it tells.
A sock puppet army plans their night,
While I pretend they don't bite!

The hallway whispers, "Take a left!"
But the cat's there, looking quite bereft.
She guards her territory like a queen,
With glances sharper than a tambourine.

Dust bunnies rally, ready to roll,
In a wild race, they steal my soul.
I trip over laughter, trip over fluff,
In this wacky world, there's never enough!

Outside the window, the world is still,
But here inside, the chaos will thrill.
With every corner, a story unfolds,
Paths unwritten, as life gently scolds.

The Ritual of Arrival

When I come home, the shoes must dance,
They leap and twist, in a happy prance.
Each step I take, they jump in glee,
Shouting, "Come on, wait for me!"

The coat rack jigs from left to right,
Hanging jackets join the merry sight.
"Welcome back!" they seem to sing,
As if they're dressed for a gala fling!

Keys jangle like a band on parade,
The fridge gives a glimmering charade.
I clap my hands, it clinks and rattles,
My kitchen's now home to wild cavales!

In this abode, the magic thrives,
Every corner hums, my heart derives.
From sill to sink, joy intertwines,
The welcome dance where laughter shines.

Footprints of the Intimate

Like cookie crumbs on a sunny floor,
Tiny tales tell of laughter galore.
Paw prints trail from the door to the hall,
Each one's a story, just wait for the call!

Footsteps echo in a playful race,
A puppet parade in our cozy space.
With every leap and hop they make,
I muse on memories, stirred by the wake.

Tiny voices giggle, whisper, and shout,
"Who left this mess?" they giggle about.
It's a treasure map for smiles and fun,
In this charming chaos, we've already won!

From hallway whispers to kitchen chews,
Each footprint sings its quirky blues.
In this shared space where joy is ripe,
Life's funny quirks are the best type.

The Unlocked Treasure

A key went missing, here we go,
I checked the fridge and found some dough.
The pantry whispered, secrets old,
In jars of jam, their stories told.

The cat looked smug, as if to say,
"This treasure hunt is just my play!"
I opened drawers, found one sock,
The mysteries of this old block!

Under the couch, a treasure map,
A nugget of gold? Just a candy wrap.
With every creak and squeak, I grinned,
This silly quest, my heart justinned.

So here I stand, amidst my loot,
Half of it food, the other a boot.
The real treasure? Laughter and cheer,
In this wild hunt, my joy is clear.

Welcome to the Quiet Place

Step on in, where whispers dwell,
A quiet nook, with tales to tell.
The clock ticks softly, a gentle tune,
While mice perform a grand festoon.

The dust bunnies dance, all in a row,
Fluffy and shy, they steal the show.
In corners, the shadows play peek-a-boo,
Who knew such fun could feel so new?

Sipping tea with a spoony grin,
Each sip brings giggles from within.
I swear there's magic in this hush,
As silence sings, and time does rush.

So take a seat, unwind your mind,
In this stillness, cheer's defined.
A quiet place where all are free,
To laugh and dream, just you and me.

An Invitation to the Untamed

Come join the fun, let's lose the reins,
In a wild world where laughter reigns.
Squirrels debate on how to prance,
While raccoons teach the art of dance.

The trees wear hats of tangled hair,
While flowers gossip without a care.
The bees throw raves, a buzzing spree,
Nature's party, come sip some tea!

A clever fox regales the crew,
With tales of mischief and what they blew.
A slip, a trip, the mud's a friend,
In this wild place, the giggles blend.

Let's climb that hill, race with the breeze,
Where fun is buried beneath the trees.
An untamed spirit, wild and free,
An invitation here awaits for thee.

Dwelling in the Hidden

In secret spots, where shadows grow,
I found a nook, come take it slow.
The coffee pot brewed a dance of steam,
And time paused in a dreamy dream.

The cushions grin, all plump and round,
Each swallow-tailed cushion made a sound.
The rug did a jig when I stepped on it,
In laughter's realm, there's no dull bit.

A hidden nook, where squirrels peek,
Plotting shenanigans, so unique.
With every tickle, and every poke,
The air is thick with cheerful joke.

So gather 'round, in this secret space,
Where giggles echo, and smiles lace.
In corners cozy, where joy is spun,
Dwell with me now, let's laugh and run!

Inviting the Unexplored

Let's open this door, it creaks and squeaks,
What wonders await behind the unique peaks.
A sock in the corner, a lost shoe or two,
And maybe a gnome who thinks he's a Jew.

Grab a flashlight, don't trip on the mat,
This place is a jungle where weird things chat.
A cat wearing glasses is reading a book,
I'm not judging him, just giving a look.

Glimpse of a rainbow, behind a small shelf,
Perhaps this old closet knows more than myself.
Adventures abound in this house full of jest,
Never know what you'll find, just humor your quest.

Exploring with laughter, what joy there is found,
From leftover pizza to toys on the ground.
Life's little quirks, swinging wide with a grin,
Let's embrace all the chaos; it's time to begin!

Navigating the Inner Landscape

Step inside this maze where thoughts collide,
Watch out for the fridge, it might try to hide.
A pickle is plotting to swim out a door,
While bananas are practicing dance on the floor.

Let's wander around, what's in that dark pot?
Maybe it's wisdom, or maybe it's snot.
A dance-off with pillows, they wiggle and sway,
Who knew thoughts could tango and frolic all day?

Laughter erupts from a mirror's sharp glance,
Reflecting my fears that've forgotten to dance.
Through hallways of giggles, past doors made of tease,
This tapestry's woven with colorful ease.

As I skip through these layers of silly surprise,
I find I'm a giant in the guesswork of lies.
So here's to the journey, a wild, wacky ride,
In the land of the mind where the fun never hides!

The Steps Before Discovery

One foot in the mess, oh what a sight,
Shoes dance and frolick, all full of delight.
A sock rebel yells, 'Time for a spin!'
While the dust bunnies cheer, 'Let the fun begin!'

Each stair has a story, each creak has a tune,
Is that an old sandwich? Or a big dancing moon?
From here to the closet, my heart starts to race,
With laughter and mayhem, I tour this strange space.

Peeking out the windows, they giggle and tease,
Little whispers of mischief drift in with the breeze.
But hey, who's that waiting beneath the first stair?
It's the ghost of my laundry, which no longer cares!

With a skip and a hop, I'm about to explore,
The chaos of life offers up so much more.
Embracing the silly, the whacky, the wild,
I'm just a small kid — life's forever the child!

Passageways of Emotion

Doors of perception swing open with glee,
Where laughter and sadness take turns for a spree.
Crossing the threshold of feelings unbound,
It's a carnival ride on a hill that's profound.

Socks filled with giggles, they trip, they fall,
With a ping-pong of joy ricocheting down the hall.
The kitchen's a symphony of flavors and quirks,
Popcorn's debating with the broccoli smirks.

A doorway to smiles or a portal to woes,
Grab the nearest sprout; let's see how it goes.
A bubble of laughter, a tear on a cheek,
Emotions flip-flopping, it's fun at the peak!

So twirl through the passages, embrace every wall,
With a wink from the garden gnome, let's have a ball!
Laughter is wisdom, and joy governs all,
In the realms of the heart, let's dance and enthrall!

The Unseen Journey

I stumbled on a doormat,
It read 'Welcome, friend!'
But tripped over my own feet,
Got lost where laughs transcend.

In my quest for hidden snacks,
I met a sock puppet sage,
He said, 'Life's a funny show,
Just don't read off the page.'

My cat was the tour guide,
With a map marked in fur,
Every twist led to mischief,
And a loud purring stir.

Eventually I found me,
In a wardrobe full of dreams,
With echoes of giggles bright,
And a heart bursting at the seams.

Invitations to the Inner Garden

The garden gate lay ajar,
With gnomes holding up signs,
'Come play among the daisies,
Just avoid the squirrels' lines.'

Each flower wore a bowtie,
And danced with great delight,
They whispered secret laughter,
In the soft glow of moonlight.

A snail with shades on strutted,
Claimed he'd just won a race,
While worms cheered in the soil,
With a ukelele's grace.

But when I tried to join in,
I ended up in a pie,
The laughter rolled like thunder,
As I waved my hands goodbye.

Quietude Beyond the Steps

I tiptoed down the hallway,
Where echoes turned to prance,
A creaky floorboard giggled,
    Inviting me to dance.

There was a chair in the corner,
    With tales it longed to tell,
It spewed out secrets softly,
    About the time I fell.

Cobwebs laughed in shadows,
Spinning tales of old delight,
Each thread a funny moment,
That sparkled in the night.

Yet outside there were noises,
Of ducks playing tag in rain,
I sighed and welcomed laughter,
    Embracing all my 'pain.'

A Gaze into the Inner Landscape

Peeking through a window,
I found a circus parade,
Clowns juggled all my worries,
And balloons seemed to cascade.

A dog was balancing treats,
While cats played mean pranks back,
The scene danced with sheer chaos,
In a colorful attack.

A mirror cracked from the laughter,
Reflected my goofy face,
I joined the jolly ruckus,
In this whimsical space.

So here's to our wild journeys,
With puns thrown in for flair,
Life's a funny carnival,
If we only dare to care.

Shades of the Unseen

Behind the curtain, a cat does spy,
Plotting adventures, oh me, oh my!
With whiskers twitching and tail in a swirl,
He dreams of conquering the whole wide world.

There's shadows dancing, but they're just the light,
A ghostly waltz, though it gives quite a fright.
Invisible specters laughing with glee,
Baking cookies for unsuspecting me!

Beneath the furniture, a treasure trove,
Dust bunnies plotting, oh how they rove!
With a wobbly chair, not a soul's at stake,
Just a dance party for the brave and the fake.

So, peek through the cracks and lend an ear,
For laughter and mischief are always near.
Life's unscripted, a curious play,
Where silliness reigns both night and day.

Crossing the Welcome Threshold

A knock on the door, a clown in disguise,
With a pie in hand and mischief in his eyes.
He shuffles right in, leaves a trail of cream,
With laughter and giggles, he starts the scheme.

The welcome mat grins, inviting the jest,
As socks on the floor play an unwelcome guest.
A tumble of shoes in a wobbly pile,
Each one holds stories, each one has style.

The kitchen's a playground, the pantry a maze,
With cereal towers, a breakfast craze.
Who knew that toast could be served on the floor,
An artful disaster, who could ask for more?

Friends gather 'round, sharing tales of delight,
As glittering confetti springs forth with might.
Each moment a giggle, each laugh a cheer,
In the warmth of the chaos, all hearts draw near.

Secrets Behind Closed Doors

Behind the door, there's a mysterious sound,
The squeak of a turtle spinning 'round and 'round.
With goggles and fins, he's ready to dive,
In the kiddie pool dreams, he feels so alive!

Wigs and odd hats hang like old friends of yore,
With tales to tell and laughter in store.
A closet of whimsy, a treasure chest bright,
Each piece a story, oh what a sight!

The dryer hums softly, a secret of fluff,
Conspiring with socks in a daring old bluff.
A sock puppet army, they plot and conspire,
While the laundry spins tales that never tire.

So peek in the shadows, embrace the unclear,
For secrets can sparkle when shared with good cheer.
Behind closed doors, life's tapestry swirls,
Full of the giggles and joy that unfurls.

A Portal to Possibility

A door creaks open, but what will we find?
A world of giggles, adventures unlined.
Pans hover by, cooking up some fun,
While the sun tickles laughter, making hearts run.

Beyond the threshold, a rainbow prance,
With jellybean clouds in a candy land dance.
Silly little creatures with shoes of bright hue,
Invite us to join in the playful view.

With whirlwinds of whimsy and doodles in flight,
Each turn is a chuckle, each laugh pure delight.
Imagination's a swing set, hungry for souls,
That dare to embrace all the possible goals.

So let's step on through to this world so askew,
Where giggles are currency and dreams come true.
In a portal of laughter, we'll twirl and we'll spin,
Celebrating the joy of our curious kin.

Echoes Linger Just Inside

Footsteps tap-dancing on the floor,
Cups clatter like they want some more.
Laughter bounces off the walls,
A party where no one calls.

The cat eyes me with a smug little grin,
As if she knows the fun I'm in.
I trip over shoes piled high,
And wonder how they reached the sky.

Leftover snacks from last night's raid,
In a bowl that's joyfully displayed.
I munch and chuckle, caught off guard,
With crumbs falling, my life's a bard.

Whispers echo in the cozy corner,
Stories shared like a friendly warner.
Who knew my heart would find a rhyme,
In a house where I'm just passing time?

An Open Invitation

The door swings wide with a goofy creak,
A welcome mat that's lost its peak.
"Come on in!" it seems to sing,
While I try to fit in my bling.

Each step is like a clumsy dance,
Where socks are paired with zero chance.
I tumble right into a wide embrace,
Of pillows soft and a smiling face.

The snacks are spread like fancy art,
I'm stuffed before I even start.
With giggles flying high and free,
Who knew chaos could feel like glee?

The air is thick, with fun and jest,
A gathering that feels like a fest.
I wave goodbye with crumbs in hand,
Wondering how this life got grand.

The Quiet Unfolding of Self

A mirror reflects not just my hair,
But secrets nested in my stare.
I wave to the self I can't outsmart,
Who giggles back with a playful heart.

In soft whispers, the quirks parade,
Like socks that never seem to fade.
I trip on thoughts that tumble and roll,
While ice cream dreams fill up my soul.

Unexpected dances in the hall,
Where shadows play and memories call.
I spin in circles, wrapped in delight,
Thinking "Who knew I could take flight?"

A journey deep with giggles and sighs,
Unfolding truths, like surprise pies.
I laugh at the mess, the blissful strife,
In this quirky, zany dance called life.

A Journey into the Echo

Every step is a chatterbox,
Unlocks a tale wrapped in paradox.
The walls hum loud with laughter bright,
As I giggle in the warming light.

I chase shadows that seem to tease,
Like puddles waiting for a breeze.
Bouncing off with a carefree cheer,
Echoing whispers I want to hear.

With each creak, the floor pulls me near,
To moments where giggles reappear.
Like popcorn popping, hearts collide,
In this amusing, wild ride.

Turning corners brings a joyful fate,
Where wit ignites and laughter waits.
I stroll through echoes, soft and wide,
And find the joy in every stride.

Threshold of Reflection

Stepping inside, I trip on the mat,
Where's my balance? Oh, fancy that!
I gaze in the mirror, it cracks a grin,
Reflections of chaos, let the fun begin!

Dust bunnies dance, they throw a ball,
They slide across the floor like a pro at the mall.
Each corner a secret, every creak a tale,
In this joyful haven, we can't help but bail!

The shoes are a crowd, they argue for space,
Mismatched and funny, they all lose the race.
I try on a boot, a clown on a spree,
Hilarity rises, oh look at me!

Here's to the chaos, the laughter it brings,
In every shadow, a chuckle that sings.
The threshold is magic, where fun meets the heart,
In the mess and the laughter, we all play a part.

Echoes in the Entryway

The door creaks open with a goofy squeak,
What's lurking beyond? Oh, just my cheek!
I peek into cabinets where dust bunnies play,
They wave goodbye as I stumble away.

Echoes of laughter chase me around,
The cat gives a wink, but won't make a sound.
I swear the clock winks as it ticks with glee,
Hurry up time, there's so much to see!

The rug does a jig, it's got moves of its own,
Each step I take feels like I'm dancing alone.
In a game of charades with my socks and the cat,
I laugh at the scene, it's all just a spat!

With memories bouncing off every wall,
The echoes remind me; I'm having a ball.
The entryway's charm, a delightful parade,
A funny reminder of laughter we've made.

Gateway to Inner Depths

Open the gate, what's hiding inside?
Oh, a rogue sock has decided to hide!
A treasure trove waits, let's see what we find,
A dinosaur cookie jar, sharp teeth, unrefined!

Plates stacked like towers, a sight to behold,
They whisper sweet secrets, both new and retold.
Each nook is a portal, each cranny a friend,
Inviting me in for a giggle to lend.

Dust motes are dancing, a swirl in the breeze,
A funny collection of forgotten keys.
With a twist and a turn, I open the door,
To a realm of laughter, oh, please give me more!

The gateway sings out, "Come play if you dare!"
I tumble right in, with joy in the air.
In the depths of the funny, I find something true,
Laughter and warmth blooming, as life bids adieu.

Unveiling the Heart's Passage

With a flick of the knob, what's brewing inside?
A circus of antics in which I confide.
Old shadows emerge with a wink and a shout,
They pull on my leg as I laugh and flout!

The fridge hums a tune, it's offbeat and grand,
Like a jester who juggles with soft-serving hand.
Each meal is a quest, on a magical ride,
And who knew a sandwich could come with such pride?

Pillows conspire on the couch to conjoin,
They plot for my comfort—a witty coin.
As I sink into laughter, the day fades away,
In this heart's passage, I choose to stay.

A parade of delights lines the quirky way,
With smiles like confetti, they brighten my day.
The unveiling of joy, a journey so bright,
In this funny old place, my heart takes flight.

Lanterns in the Shadows

A lantern flickers, keeps me awake,
Who knew the cookies could give me a break?
Chasing shadows, I giggle and sway,
As the dogs plot a heist—oh, what a day!

The fridge hums secrets, it has no shame,
My midnight snack habit, oh what a game!
In the pantry, I find treasures galore,
With each tiny crumb, I always want more!

While the cat watches with a judgmental glare,
I'm just a thief, with food everywhere!
Stealing from cupboards like it's a spree,
Who knew adventures were so tasty for me?

The night wears on, but I wear a grin,
Guess it's not over till the cookie jar's thin!
So I'll dance in the dark, in my silly disguise,
With laughter echoing, 'til the morning sun rise!

Veils of the Uncharted Heart

A heart beats gently, but oh so sly,
Like a kitten with yarn, oh my, oh my!
Each secret wrapped like a gift of delight,
What is this feeling? It can't be polite!

With giggles and whispers that dance in the air,
I navigate feelings with fancy and flair.
Like a puppy with shoes, I clamor around,
Graceful? Perhaps not, but joy knows no bounds!

Could it be love or just cottage cheese?
Confusion is funny, a tickle, a tease.
Uncharted, unfiltered, my heart takes a leap,
With laughter emerging from all of this heap!

A navigation map drawn in spaghetti strings,
With all my emotions, oh the chaos it brings!
So here's to the veils, as silly as they be,
I'll laugh through the maze and be utterly free!

The Welcome Silence

A quiet so lovely, like socks with no feet,
Silence is golden, or so they repeat.
Yet in this still moment, a sneeze from the cat,
Breaks the calm echo, oh, how absurd is that!

In the pause, the clock tick-tocks in a jest,
My mind wanders off, and I start to jest.
Imagining elves in a worldwide parade,
Dancing with slippers, how plans are portrayed!

A soft little hum of the fridge in the back,
Makes me ponder how pets have no knack.
For this welcome silence, so treasured and rare,
Funny how life stirs the space in mid-air!

So here's to the quiet, my sweet little friend,
Who knows where it leads? On that, we depend.
May laughter arise from the depths of this hush,
And may each little silence add joy to the rush!

Halls of Memory's Embrace

In the halls of my mind, where memories play,
An old rubber chicken leads the ballet.
Twisting and turning, it squeaks with such flair,
How did it get there? I don't have a care!

Old photos are dancing, like socks in a whirl,
Grandma with shades and a bright, fearless girl.
With laughter erupting from times gone before,
Silly mischief lives—who could ask for more?

Echoes of laughter float high on the breeze,
While whispers of nonsense bring me to my knees.
In this grand hall of quirks, I twirl with delight,
The ghosts of my past put a smile on the night!

So here's to the memories wrapped in this yarn,
Each twist tells a story, like a good luck charm.
May the laughter we conjure be warm and embrace,
In the whimsical halls, may we forever find grace!

Shadows Embracing the Light

In the corner, dust bunnies dance,
They giggle at my clumsy prance.
They whisper secrets, cheeky and bright,
As I trip over my shoes—what a sight!

The sunbeams tease the curtains wide,
While I chase my shadow, hoping to hide.
It flickers and pops like it's got a mind,
Laughing as it leaves my sanity behind.

A cat's patrolling with a regal air,
Laughing softly at my disheveled hair.
With every step, the floorboards creak,
The house plays games, a bit of a sneak.

So here I am, the jester sprawled,
In the land of shadows, I've been enthralled.
Embracing the light, what a noble quest,
If only my socks would pass the test!

Heartbeats Beyond the Entrance

The door swings wide with a creaky scream,
I stumble forward, lost in a dream.
Heart racing faster than a caffeinated bat,
What's waiting inside? A shoe or a cat?

The welcome mat whispers my secret news,
It's seen my last dancing, in fuzzy shoes.
I strut through like royalty stepping on confetti,
Only to trip—my dignity unsteady.

The clock is ticking; time will not wait,
It's bound to berate me for being late.
I'm greeted by laughter, a chorus so spry,
My missteps are legends, oh me, oh my!

As I gather myself, I'm the punchline of jokes,
While family members laugh and poke.
With heartbeats throbbing, I learn my role,
A blend of humor in each little fold.

Whispers of the Threshold

A breeze brushes past with a giggling sigh,
As I fumble and bumble, oh my, oh my!
The threshold, a stage, I make my debut,
While the doorframe giggles and joins in too.

Mystery carpets underfoot begin to sway,
Tickling my toes as I stumble in play.
The couch waves back with a soft, knowing glance,
As if it remembers my last epic dance.

Lamp shades flicker, they're joining the fun,
Winking at me as I'm on the run.
With every corner, laughter spills out,
The whispers are loud, sparking joy, no doubt.

So in I tumble with grace like a goat,
Spinning and twirling, I lose my coat.
In this place, a banquet of chuckles awaits,
Like a carnival ride, full of jovial fates!

Beyond the Welcome Mat

Past the threshold, where shenanigans lie,
The mat shakes its fibers, almost to cry.
It's been trampled on too many times to count,
Yet here I am, missing my entrance mount.

The coat rack sways, jealous of my style,
"Hung up your dreams?" it asks with a smile.
As hats tumble down in an avalanche spin,
They whisper in jest, 'Hey, let the fun begin!'

Pictures on walls seem to snicker and grin,
Reflecting my chaos, it's clear I can't win.
They shake their frames as I dive for the seat,
It's a comedy club without missing a beat.

So come all you shadows, and join in the jest,
In this lively abode, you'll find laughter at best.
Beyond the welcome mat, where joy is the start,
Life's little surprises tickle the heart!

Where Dusk Meets Dawn

When twilight whispers, watch me roam,
With socks askew, I stumble home.
The cat just stares, as if to joke,
My shadow dances, like a cloak.

In the hallway, I trip on shoes,
The light in the fridge reveals my blues.
Yet with a grin, I save the day,
And promptly spill my juice in dismay.

Reflecting laughter on the wall,
I chat with ghosts who used to fall.
Their chuckles bounce within my head,
As I munch crumbs left of toast, instead.

A colorful mess, this life is grand,
With doodles drawn by an invisible hand.
As dusk meets dawn, what silly spree,
To find adventure just being me!

Subtle Tones of Reflection

The mirror chuckles at my hair,
It dances wildly, without a care.
I grimace back, what's with this style?
It screams for help, but stays awhile.

Coffee cup in hand, I take a chance,
Trip on a rug, it seems to prance.
My plants all watch with leafy grins,
As muddy shoes declare my sins.

Reflections twist, they laugh and play,
As I ponder where to hide away.
In every crack, the giggles grow,
As wisdom scoffs at what I know.

With every stumble, every fall,
The walls just seem to have a ball.
In subtle tones, they hum my tune,
Turning chaos into a cartoon.

The Heartbeat of Entry

Opening the door, what do I find?
A wiggly dog, a curious mind.
It leaps like a cloud, fluffy and bright,
While I dodge the mud with all my might.

Inside, the socks have staged a coup,
They giggle loudly, they spell out "boo!"
A playful cat strikes a pose so grand,
As I try to figure where they stand.

My heart beats fast, it's quite absurd,
With all this madness, it's hard to be heard.
Laughter echoes from room to room,
In this cozy chaos, I find my bloom.

Each moment a dance, each corner a jest,
In this odd little world, I feel so blessed.
The heartbeat of entry is pure delight,
With animals plotting the silliest night!

An Opened Chest

An opened chest, buried treasures reveal,
Dusty old socks should not be a meal.
With items misplaced, some toys gone rogue,
Every dive in there feels like a vogue.

In a forgotten box, a jester's hat,
It fits just right, I feel like a brat.
Spinning around, I play the fool,
Cause life's a stage and I rule the school.

The buttons jump and the marbles roll,
A quirky pebble becomes my goal.
With whispers of laughter, the memories stir,
As I trip on hidden dreams that were fur.

In that opened chest, joy is found,
Every silly item holds laughter unbound.
So here's to the treasures and the happiness spun,
In the randomness of life, we all have our fun!

The Sanctuary of Soft Murmurs

In the closet, old socks reside,
Whispers shared, secrets confide.
Teddy bears chuckle, it seems,
As they ponder their childhood dreams.

Dust bunnies dance, they roam free,
Playing hide-and-seek, just like me.
With coffee mugs as their thrones,
They rule the kingdom of soft tones.

Through Cracks of the Known

In a garden, weeds wear crowns,
Eavesdropping on all the towns.
A squirrel steals snacks with pure glee,
Claiming nuts as royalty.

Raccoons hold meetings late at night,
Discussing strategies, oh what a sight!
With twinkling eyes, they scheme their plans,
While a cat judges from the pans.

The Boundary of Reality

In kitchens, pots sing a tune,
While pancakes jump like they're on the moon.
The fridge hums a grumpy song,
Reminding us where we belong.

Spaghetti dances, twirls in the air,
With meatballs trying to show flair.
In this realm where laughter's the key,
Cooking's a whimsical spree!

Gazing Through the Veil

Peeking through, a curious cat,
Wonders where all the humans sat.
With paw on the window, it dreams wide,
Of fish in ponds, and a wild ride.

The curtains flutter, the wind laughs,
As chairs plot their silly gaffes.
Every creak tells a story, oh so bold,
Of chairs that dance in twilight gold.

When Walls Speak

When walls begin to murmur,
With secrets of the past,
I tiptoe past the dog,
And pray he's not a blast.

The fridge squeaks out its stories,
Of leftovers long gone,
While curtains plot their heists,
In the early light of dawn.

The floorboards creak in laughter,
As I shuffle my spaghetti,
They know of all my antics,
And still they stay unsteady.

Each room a running joke,
With echoes made of cheer,
In the house we share together,
I wipe away a tear.

Hidden Rooms of the Heart

Beneath the staircase lies a gem,
A sock, a shoe, a pen,
I knew it was a treasure,
But can't recall when.

In closets filled with chaos,
With coats from days gone past,
I search for lost adventures,
And stuff them all in fast.

Behind each door is mayhem,
With giggles trapped inside,
Even the old vacuum laughs,
As I attempt to hide.

A treasure trove of memories,
With laughter steeped in heart,
In every hidden corner,
A silly work of art.

Beyond the Sill of Silence

The window attracts whispers,
Of neighbors' loud disputes,
I listen close for secrets,
Like eavesdropping roots.

The curtain flutters lightly,
As gossip fills the air,
I laugh along the edges,
As if I'm really there.

With every clink of teacups,
New tales unfold in time,
From friendship to the awkward,
Like poorly sung a rhyme.

So weird and wacky moments,
Are tucked within that frame,
Beyond a simple window,
All hearts are just the same.

A Journey Within the Frame

I hung a painting crookedly,
It winks at anyone,
A journey through abstract,
Where logic is just fun.

Its colors clash and sparkle,
Like jellybeans in mid-flight,
I ponder its intention,
Was it baked with pure delight?

The frame speaks in a whisper,
With sarcasm so bright,
I chuckle at the shadows,
That dance in soft moonlight.

An explorer of the nonsense,
I step into the gleam,
Each glance a funny story,
Like laughter in a dream.

Fragments Behind the Veil

A riddle wrapped in a sock,
Each day's a giggle, a tickle, a mock.
Secrets stored in the cookie jar,
Winks shared under a chocolate bar.

Laughter echoes in the quiet space,
Where shadows dance with a silly grace.
A couch that swallows socks and dreams,
And whispers of pies and joyful screams.

Whispers from the Hallway

A creaky floor on a wobbly night,
Where cats hold council, and ghosts take flight.
Jokes hidden behind a curtain's sway,
As time slips by in a comedic way.

A light bulb flickers, a wink in the dark,
With punchlines waiting—a scholastic lark.
The toaster's puns are perfectly toast,
With laughter serving bubbly, at most.

Beyond the Welcome

A doormat yawns with a dusty grin,
While shoes parade like a goofy kin.
Hats hang low, yet spirits so high,
Where every glance unlocks a pie.

Inside the chaos, a symphony hums,
With pots that dance to the beat of drums.
Silly antics, from ceiling to floor,
Each chuckle a tale behind an old door.

The Journey of Unseen Horizons

A map drawn in crayon with zig-zag lines,
Adventure awaits in the weirdest designs.
Cupcakes lead to wild, wandering streams,
Each nibble a laughter, a playful dream.

Balloons carry giggles and butterflies,
In this realm where the humor flies.
Every corner holds a curious quirk,
On this goofy path, where oddities lurk.

Steps on the Path of Being

Each footstep sounds a silly tune,
A dance we do beneath the moon.
With every glance we see the quirks,
Life slips and slides as laughter lurks.

When shadows stretch in playful spree,
I trip and tumble, oh woe is me!
Each stumble's just a forward leap,
So giggle loud, don't dare to weep.

In comic poses, we find our way,
On crazy avenues, we sway.
With spirits high, we skip and hop,
The journey's fun, we can't just stop.

So keep those smiles, let joy preside,
Embrace the odd, let hearts abide.
For every twist and turn we find,
A treasure lies, unconfined.

Reflections in the Entryway

In mirrors shaped like silly doughnuts,
I see my smile that clearly struts.
A wink and nudge to those who glare,
Makes it absurd, oh what a flare!

The entryway is a stage so grand,
Where sock puppets take the stand.
With laughter echoing off the walls,
We twirl and leap, the spirit calls.

A portrait of my wildest hair,
It's not just art, it's pure debonair.
Each reflection brings another jest,
I'm a comic, and I know it best!

As guests arrive, they chuckle too,
Expecting fun with every cue.
For life's too short to take a toll,
Let humor ignite and fill our soul!

Open Spaces of the Spirit

Wide open spaces, yet no one's there,
Just my thoughts, still floating in air.
A cake of dreams with icing bright,
Who knew spirits could be such a sight?

I leap like bees from flower to bee,
Each vision flits, silly and free.
With jester hats and rubber shoes,
I bounce through life with no real cues.

The winds of whimsy lift me high,
While rainbows paint the perfect sky.
In corners strange, where giggles roam,
I find the key, I make it home.

So in this space, where laughter reigns,
Let silliness run through our veins.
For open hearts can surely see,
The joys of life in quirky glee!

The Threshold of Self

At the edge of me, quite bizarre,
I find my jests, they shine like stars.
A step ahead, I laugh and frown,
The door swings wide; it's upside down!

With every peek, a new surprise,
The cat in hats with googly eyes.
I wear a smile, a cozy jest,
In this domain, I'm truly blessed.

The welcome mat's an anxious grin,
It begs you to come join the din.
With silliness as our best friend,
We twirl together, 'round the bend.

So let's embrace this playful hue,
A world where laughter always grew.
For in this space, where souls unite,
We find our joy in jestful flight!

www.ingramcontent.com/pod-product-compliance
Lightning Source LLC
Chambersburg PA
CBHW051733290426
43661CB00123B/253